Squirt

A True Story of
an Unforgettable Lamb

Deb Hetle

ISBN: Number

E-Book: 978-1-969066-47-4

Paperback: 978-1-969066-48-1

Hardcover: 978-1-969066-49-8

Published by
Columbus Book Publishers
www.columbusbookpublishers.com

Printed in the United States of America

Dedication

This book is dedicated to my family:

I dedicate it to my parents, Mel and Faye Schneider, for first introducing me to the wonderful world of woolies. You taught me to love them, to care for them, to see them as personalities and pets and not just as animals.

I dedicate it to my wonderful husband Paul and my three children, Philip, April and Gina. Paul, you were willing to take a plunge with me into the lively land of lambing even when you had never been around a sheep before. We learned and grew together, and it continues to be an adventure we have never regretted. When you were children, you three Hetles helped me to see lambs through the eyes of a child and to see the child-likeness that is in each one of them, young and old. To see your excitement added zest to this adventure.

And, most importantly, I dedicate this book to God, for it is He who has tenderly given us insight into the loving heart and soul of the Shepherd and into the mind and desperate helplessness of the Sheep. So many times, Lord,

You have revealed to us the truth that we are like sheep and constantly reminded us of your immeasurable love for us. You gave us special sheep, each hand-picked by You, to teach us lessons that brought parts of your Scripture alive in a way we would not have otherwise understood. Our flock taught us in the same way that the sheep of Your flock teach each other. For this I gratefully and humbly say, Thank You for the opportunity to be a shepherd.

Acknowledgment

This book is the culmination of a journey that began so many years ago. But once I started down the path to chronicle the stories and wooly characters which made up these memories, a team of cheerleaders kept me moving even when I became distracted for a long while.

My parents, Mel and Faye Schneider, my first "shepherds"—you introduced me to those first sweet bottle lambs, and to Jesus. Heaven is sweeter because you are face to face with the true Shepherd now.

Paul, my dear husband, you were willing to plunge into raising sheep when it was a new experience for you. You have pushed me along and believed in this book and me. I couldn't have finished it without your encouragement.

Philip Hetle, April Hetle Larson, and Gina Hetle Mees—my three "lambs." You are a big part of most of these memories, so I am happy to share them with you once again as well as with our 7 grandchildren. Owen, thanks for the last-minute push that got me going again!

Mia Werger, a new friend, thank you for sharing your photo of this precious lamb with me.

Belva Wedel, only God and I know how much your gentle nudges have meant to me. Even when distance separated us, your encouraging words continued to echo through my mind. I am forever grateful for you.

Thank you to many friends who encouraged me along this journey. You are all gifts from God.

About the Book

This is a true story about a very special lamb and how God used him in our lives in a most unforgettable way. God gave us this tiny gift as a modern-day parable of Christ's coming to earth in human form as a tiny babe to live among us, love us, teach us, and become the final sacrificial Lamb to take away our sins. This experience with Squirt gave us a new perspective of Christ's birth, death and resurrection that we will never forget.

The story of Squirt will warm your heart, make you smile, and bring you into a new and deeper love for Jesus, our eternal Lamb.

About the Author

My love for animals and the outdoors began at age 6 when my family moved to a farm in Central South Dakota. I was first introduced to a variety of farm animals, each winning a place in my heart. But around age 12, my two sisters, brother and I entered the world of bottle lambs, and my passion for sheep grew quickly. They were more than a 4-H project and responsibility; they were my friends.

Then after college and marriage, my husband Paul and I bought our own small farm. Within a year sheep entered our lives again and stayed for the next 22 years. Our three children—Philip, April and Gina, grew up alongside them, learning responsibility, life lessons, and the heart of a shepherd.

Even more importantly, however, my love for Jesus Christ as my Savior and Friend began around age 9. He brought peace and forgiveness to my searching heart and a new way of life. As my commitment to Him grew and my desire to know what He said in the Bible, the passages that called us His sheep and Jesus our Good Shepherd jumped off the page and into my soul. It was then that I began connecting the dots between our experiences with these defenseless animals and what the Bible said about my own human condition outlined in the Bible. Before our eyes, the passages came to life in our flock. I began recording these experiences and how God revealed His heart through them. I also began to realize that every detail of my life is important to Him, His precious lamb.

Thus, this book began as simply a desire to compile these memories and lessons for our kids and grandchildren so as not to lose them forever, as in Deuteronomy 4:9: *"Only be careful and watch yourselves closely so that you do not forget the things your eyes have seen or let them fade from your heart as long as you live. Teach them to your children and to their children after them."*

But I sincerely hope and pray that each reader may find a connection between his or her heart and that of the Good Shepherd, our Lord Jesus. To God be the glory!

Table of Contents

Chapter 1 A Tiny Babe 1

Chapter 2 A Big Surprise.......................................4

Chapter 3 A New Family 6

Chapter 4 A New Love 9

Chapter 5 A Second Chance 12

Chapter 6 A New Friend.....................................16

Chapter 7 Saying Good-bye................................21

Chapter 8 A New Perspective.............................23

Chapter 9 A New Life in Christ...........................26

Section 2 The Sheep of His Pasture 29

Introduction...31

Chapter 1 The Shepherd in Training.....................33

Chapter 2 The Practice Field...............................36

Chapter 3 The Flock..38

Chapter 4 The Lessons Learned..........................49

Chapter 5 The Shepherd's Psalm 71

Chapter 6 The Big Question 73

Chapter 1
A Tiny Babe

It was a cold and snowy March afternoon in 1999. The sun made one last effort to break through the heavy clouds casting its last glance on our part of the world before tucking away at the end of another day. It was going to be a very cold night.

Our lambing season had been going pretty well. With the help of our children, Philip, April and Gina, the north side of the barn had been filled with little square pens, each a miniature maternity ward to a new mother sheep known as a ewe (pronounced "you") and her newborn lambs. Often these mommies had twins or even triplets and were fiercely protective of the tiny babies who stayed cuddled close to their mother's side which provided warmth and safety.

Paul and our son Philip checked the sheep one last time at the end of this Saturday. "Dad," Phil called to Paul who was inside the barn wrapping up the feeding. "Come out here quick. There's one that just lambed outside." As Paul stuck his head out of the barn door and gazed across the small corral where the flock could spend the afternoons, he sighed in disappointment.

Squirt came into the world a little prematurely on that cold, early March evening. He was one of twins born to a first-time-mom ewe who did not have the slightest idea what to do with the little creature writhing on the ground at her feet, nor did she want to know. Squirt's twin was just a tiny envelope of pink skin with a head and tiny legs, much too deformed to take even that first gasp of breath. But Squirt, not much more in substance than his lifeless twin, had a purpose. A future. An adventure waiting. A world to affect. He was so tiny that he fit snugly into two hands.

Squirt tried hard to breathe. After placing Squirt and his reluctant mother into a pen, Paul and Phil did everything they could to keep him alive. They rubbed him and massaged his chest to encourage him to breathe. They cleared his airway of fluids so there was nothing in the way, but this weak little creature just didn't have the strength to breathe on his own.

A Tiny Babe

"Philip, there comes a time when we just have to stop and let go. We did all we could. This one's just too premature and weak to live. Let's go to the house." Paul knew these were important life lessons for a son who was becoming a man and learning that letting go was part of life too. They turned off the heat lamp that hung over the dying lamb and left him alone in the dark with his mother who wanted nothing to do with him. He was a small loss.

Chapter 2
A Big Surprise

Paul and I took turns getting up early in the mornings to check the sheep for new babies. The next morning, Sunday, was my turn. The snow made a wonderful crunching sound as I made my way through the darkness to the barn. As I entered the barn my gaze went immediately to the pen in the corner, and a wave of sadness caught in my heart.

I peeked into the pen where Squirt had been left, prepared to carry his little lifeless body out of the barn. There, however, in a most helpless heap, lay little Squirt, very much alive! His head was up, he was crying his little lungs out and trying desperately to get up on scrawny legs that were too weak to lift him. I could not believe my eyes! I picked him up in my hand and held him up to his mother's milk supply so he could try to nurse. He was so short that he was unable to reach even from a standing position, so I just held him there as he gratefully gorged himself on his first meal of rich warm milk. Then I tucked him inside my coat against my body and zipped the coat again to keep him warm for the trip to the house.

As I stepped into our kitchen I called out, "Hey, everybody, get up and look at this!"

Pretty soon Paul and three sleepy kids showed up in the kitchen to see what the noise was about. As I unzipped my coat a dirty tiny head popped out with wide curious eyes and perky ears. Immediately he gave a feeble greeting as if to announce, "I changed my mind! Think I'll stick around."

Imagine our excitement over this tiny lamb that was left for dead. It reminds me of the story in the Bible where the Apostle Paul had been stoned, dragged out of the city, and left for dead, but God had a bigger plan for him for all of us to learn from.

"[19]...They stoned Paul and dragged him outside the city, thinking he was dead. [20]But after the disciples had gathered around him, he got up and went back into the city. The next day he and Barnabas left for Derbe. [21]They preached the good news in that city and won a large number of disciples."

Acts 14:19-21

Chapter 3
A New Family

Since Squirt was determined to live even in his most fragile state, he needed to be bottle fed an ounce of milk at least every two hours. Since this was Sunday and tomorrow we would all be going off to school or work, a decision had to be made about his care. My sister, Karen, who lived in town, had mentioned to me that she wanted to keep a bottle lamb for a week or two so that her small children could experience caring for bottle lambs. I called her and told her we had a case for her, should she choose to accept it, but it was going to be demanding and life expectancy was not promising. She gladly accepted the challenge and we sent him to Karen's house in a 15-gallon tub.

He still was too weak to stand, and, having barely any wool and still being dirty and smelly as he was when he came into this world, he made a pitiful sight. Karen figured that her children needed to learn about death as well as life, so she took him home.

Two days later Karen called me to report on Squirt, as her children had named him. She had diligently fed him every two hours. She had bathed him and he was now white as snow.

That sounds like what God says about our condition. We come into this world as sinful creatures. In life we are dirty, stained and blemished by our sin. However, if we accept God's gift of salvation and forgiveness provided by Jesus' death on the cross, He washes us white as snow.

"Though your sins are like scarlet, they shall be white as snow; though they be red as crimson, they shall be like wool."

Isaiah 1:18

Squirt was already jumping out of the tub so they made him a little pen in the basement. He spent two and a half blissful weeks at Karen's house. During that time, she put a "diaper" around his middle and he had the run of the house. As he chased her little children through the house, they squealed and giggled. They had such a great time with him.

With her tender care, he thrived in a way I never thought possible on that cold Sunday morning.

Chapter 4
A New Love

Soon, however, Squirt was outgrowing his pen and his welcome there. It was time for him to return to the farm where he could join the other sheep, or so we thought.

Our family had fixed a comfortable and cozy pen for Squirt in the barn. After bedding it deeply with clean straw, we placed Squirt in his new home. "We'll keep you in here for a couple of weeks and then you can run with the other sheep. Okay?" We tried to reassure Squirt (and maybe even ourselves) that this was best for him. He bleated and cried when we put him down on the straw.

Within a few minutes he had wriggled his way out of this little pen and was trying to follow us back to the house again. Another couple of failed attempts, and we soon discovered that he preferred being in the house with all the other "people" he loved.

Thus, it happened that whenever we were in the house so was Squirt. He slept on my feet as I washed the dishes. When we sat in the living room to watch TV, he jumped up in a lap and slept. Wherever Philip was, Squirt was curled up beside him, contented and peaceful.

Oh, to be that dedicated to spending time with our Heavenly Shepherd. To experience that closeness and oneness with Jesus is to be truly content and safe and at peace. Too often we just want to go our own way and end up missing out on that peace.

Squirt made a wonderful house pet. This amazing little lamb was very careful to never potty in the house as Karen and her family had succeeded in house-training him. He did not leave a mess when he was eating. He did not scratch, bite, attack, tear at the furniture, lick himself in disgusting places, or shed. Weekly baths kept him clean and fresh smelling, too.

A New Love

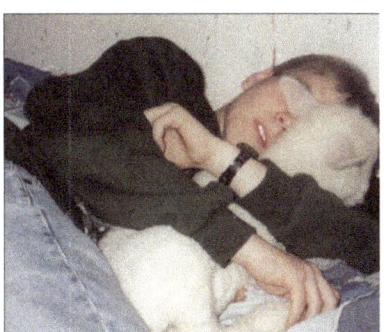

Chapter 5
A Second Chance

One morning Paul got in his car to leave for work. As he was driving out of the yard, he was unaware that Squirt had followed him out of the garage and was now chasing him down the driveway "baa"-ing for him not to leave. Suddenly Paul felt a sickening bump under his wheels. He quickly got out of the car to see what had happened. His heart sank as he saw Squirt lying in the road struggling to move. Horror and sadness swept over him as he realized he had driven over Squirt's back legs and hips. The lamb was alive but obviously very wounded.

Philip, April, Gina and I were in the kitchen finishing breakfast and getting ready for school when Paul walked back into the house carrying the hurt lamb. The look on Paul's face showed that he felt as much pain about this as did the lamb.

A Second Chance

"Will he live? Can we help him?" The kids fired questions of concern for this lamb they had grown to love as we gently placed him on a rug in the kitchen.

"Well," replied Paul in a quiet reassuring voice, "if any lamb could pull through this, it would be Squirt. He was 'dead' once and lived; maybe he can do it again." I remember looking at Paul's eyes and we shared a glance that expressed doubt and hope at the same time. "We'll just have to see."

Soon our children left for school and I was alone to care for Squirt. He picked up his head and bleated a little. His eyes were clear and alert, and he seemed to want his morning bottle of milk. As I prepared it for him, I said to myself through tears, "At least he will die with a full tummy." He gratefully downed the milk and I was a tiny bit hopeful.

A few minutes later he urinated on the rug. His urine was thick red with clotted blood, which I assumed indicated serious internal injuries. With my tiny spark of hope reduced to a smoldering cinder, I committed to just hold him and try to make him comfortable.

Squirt

During that day as I held him, fed him, petted him, loved him, I began to have a sense of how much God cares for us when we are down and hurting and how it breaks His heart to see us go through trials and agony. We are like sheep. We are helpless, hopeless creatures without His loving hand to guide us. We are completely dependent upon Him for every breath we take and every beat of our heart. Yet we go on living like we are in control of our destiny, like we are all we need, like we have no need of a Savior to pull us out of the pit of Satan's grasp, like our lives are in our hands.

When He calls us His "sheep," His voice is filled with gentle, overwhelming and all-consuming love and protection that comes flowing out of His heart to cover and surround us and draw us to Himself. He wants to make us whole. He wants to give us life. He loves us more than we even love our children and certainly more than we cared about Squirt.

The next day Squirt was still alive. He continued to eat happily and his urine eventually cleared of the blood. For three days he lay on that rug in the kitchen unable to stand. Several times a day we lifted him to a standing position to see if he was getting stronger. Amazingly, little by little he was able to stand again. Soon he could hop on three legs, and a couple of weeks later he was back on all four feet and doing well. He was truly a survivor!

Squirt spent a total of about five weeks living in our house. Eventually his wool grew in soft and white, and the house was too warm for him. It was time for him to move outside. He never did accept the fact that he could possibly be related to those smelly dirty critters out in the barnyard and preferred to lie on the steps by the door like a pet dog does. In fact, we often found him lying by the chicken house fence watching the chickens and listening to their cackling conversations. He eventually had a straw bed in the granary near the house where he could come and go freely.

Chapter 6
A New Friend

Then came the day when the sheep became the shepherd.

"You have heard me teach things that have been confirmed by many reliable witnesses. Now teach these truths to other trustworthy people who will be able to pass them on to others."

2 Timothy 2:2 (NLT)

Discipleship: To help a person come to the point of maturity in Christ where he or she can then disciple another, allowing the cycle to continue.

Each of us reading this story has been a "Squirt" sometime in life. Our parents, our teachers, our pastors, all those who care about us invest time and energy to help "grow us up" to be responsible and mature. God puts shepherds in our lives to help us grow in our love relationship with Him so that we can then reach out and be shepherds to other lambs who need Jesus. And on it goes, generation after generation.

"Be careful never to forget what you yourself have seen. Do not let these memories escape from your mind as long as you live! Be sure to pass them on to your children and to your grandchildren."

Deuteronomy 4:9 (NLT)

Well, back to when our little sheep became the shepherd.

There is a disease that young lambs get called white muscle disease, a vitamin E deficiency that causes extreme weakness in the legs to the point where the lamb cannot stand or walk. We had had several lambs with this problem previously but were never able to save them.

Sheep are social creatures, and if one becomes isolated from the rest it will just deteriorate and eventually die. The affected lamb cannot walk and is left behind by the others. Even with food available, the sick lamb fails to thrive and is lost. We have even seen the other sheep trample the weak animal in their greed to be the first to the trough.

Sounds a lot like humans, doesn't it? Sometimes we are so focused on our goals and our plans that we do not take the time to notice when others around us are discouraged or hurting or in need of a friend. Look around and see if there is someone nearby who may be lonely, someone who needs a friend who cares.

At this time, we had a lamb that became paralyzed with white muscle disease in all four legs. We quickly decided that her only chance was to come to the granary and live with Squirt where she would have company without the risk of being trampled. Squirt quickly accepted his new friend, but we were totally unprepared for his response to her.

Squirt immediately became her protector. Our cats also called the granary home. This had been acceptable to Squirt until Sammi, as we named her, moved in. Now we watched him stay by her side at all times. However, if a cat came into the building Squirt butted it all the way out the door and chased it up to the house. Then he returned to take his place at Sammi's side. We watched him do that countless times over the next couple of weeks. Sammi ate well and looked happy, but she still could not get up.

Then one day as our family was out in the yard, we saw Squirt come out of the granary a few steps, then stop to look back and call to Sammi. To our surprise, a few moments later Sammi emerged. Standing only on her "knees" in front and pushing herself along with weak back legs, she scooted along a few inches at a time. Squirt moved out ahead of her a short distance, then looked back and gave a soft "baa" as if to say, "You can do it, don't give up." After a few minutes of such exertion, Sammi collapsed to the ground again to rest and Squirt went back to lie at her side.

"Did you see that?" our kids exclaimed in disbelief. We watched in amazement! Our helpless little lamb, left for dead in the barn, was now the shepherd reaching out to another helpless lamb with a healing touch we were not capable of giving.

Still the protector from the cats, we watched Squirt work with Sammi day after day until the day finally came that she was strong enough to emerge from the granary on all four legs, wobbly but standing. We threw a party! We enjoyed cake while Squirt and Sammi enjoyed an extra scoop of corn. It was a most amazing victory and something we still marvel about. Eventually Sammi completely recovered and the two frolicked all over the yard.

In this world there are many hurting people we could reach out to. Maybe this is the time God is asking us to become a shepherd to others around us. There are lost, sick and dying souls everywhere we look. I pray that God would open my eyes to a "Sammi" He has prepared for me to reach out to.

Chapter 7
Saying Good-bye

People often asked us at that time what we would do with Squirt when he grew up. Would we sell him with the other fattened lambs? Our response was always that he would live here until he died here, which is exactly what he did.

When he was only about three months old we were outside in the yard in the evening, and I noticed that he was already lying in his straw pen in the granary, a strange thing for him to be doing so early in the evening. When I checked on him, he was grinding his teeth and grunting, a sure sign of extreme pain in a sheep. Since it was evening and a veterinarian would not be available until the next morning, we checked him over and gave him some medicine. We still did not know what was wrong but tried to make him comfortable.

Squirt

When I sat down beside him on the floor of the granary, he came and lay across my lap like he had done weeks before when he was a house lamb. Once again, he just wanted to be near the shepherd.

As our family held him and petted him that night, Sammi came and lay down under his head as he had done for her so many times. Then, as the cats came in to investigate, Sammi butted them all the way out and to the house before returning to her spot at his head. She repeated this act of devotion several times in the next hour while we held him. When night came we put him back on the straw and left the two of them, hoping things would be better in the morning.

But the next morning we found Squirt's lifeless body lying in his pen with Sammi at his side. We suspect that his earlier injuries by the car caused an internal blockage or problem that just now reared its ugly head. We buried Squirt and put Sammi back with the other sheep where she thrived. That was a very sad day.

Chapter 8
A New Perspective

Now, what does all this have to do with Christmas and Easter and Jesus the sacrificial Lamb?

During the time that Squirt lived in our home, John and Alice Barcus, missionary friends of ours, came to our house for a meal. We had put Squirt out in the garage to stay out of the way. However, when John and Alice learned about him, they wanted him to come in the house and be with us. Then John told us something that completely changed the way we look at our experience with Squirt.

John told us that when the Jews sacrificed the Passover lamb, it came to live with them in their home for a period of time. During that time it became a part of their family, their pet. They washed it so it was white as snow and without spot or blemish. They came to love it affectionately - and then they gave it up to be killed as a sacrifice for their sins.

That thought broke my heart. I felt the pain it would have caused to have lived with Squirt like we did, only to offer him to be killed as a sacrificial lamb. But that is exactly what God did for us. He loved us so much that He sent his one and only Son, Jesus, whom He loved, into this world to live among us.

> *"For God so loved the world that He gave His one and only Son, that whoever believes in Him shall not perish but have eternal life."* **John 3:16**

> *"The Word (Jesus) became flesh and made his dwelling among us. We have seen His glory, the glory of the One and Only, who came from the Father, full of grace and truth."* **John 1:14**

> *"Jesus, being in very nature God, did not regard equality with God a thing to be held onto but emptied Himself taking the very nature of a servant. And being found in appearance as a man, He humbled Himself and became obedient to death, even death on a cross."* **Philippians 2:5-8**

Jesus, the Lamb of God, came as a helpless baby to a manger of hay. He came with a purpose and a plan to bring hope, love and forgiveness of sins to every person. He lived a perfect sinless life. He healed the sick, taught us how to live and love, forgave those who wanted freedom from their sins, brought peace to those who knew no peace, showed us perfect love, and was loved back by many. Then He became the final sacrifice so His blood could cover the death penalty for our sins forever. The Bible calls him the Lamb of God who came to take away the sins of the world (John 1:29).

Yes, "We all like sheep have gone astray. Each of us has turned to his own way; and the Lord has laid on Him the sin of us all." **Isaiah 53:6**

Chapter 9
A New Life in Christ

One of the biggest frustrations of being a shepherd is dealing with bottle lambs. These unfortunate babies are the ones who have lost their mothers or have been rejected by them. We put them in a pen together with other bottle lambs so we can take care of them and help them grow up to be strong and healthy. We come to them with the life-giving milk in a bottle. Some accept it gratefully and thrive, but there are those who will fight every attempt we make to bring them a chance at life. They fight the nipple of the bottle and fight the protecting hands that offer help. If they fight long enough, they will eventually die.

Dear Reader, if you have never accepted Christ's gift of salvation and forgiveness of your sins, do not wait. The Bible tells us that *"Your enemy, the devil, prowls about like a roaring lion looking for someone to devour." (I Peter 5:8).* If you are one of those lambs who has not yet surrendered control of your life to the One who offers eternal life, now is the time. Let Him be your Shepherd before it is too late.

"I (Jesus) have come that they may have life, and have it abundantly. I am the Good Shepherd. The Good Shepherd lays down his life for the sheep." **John 10:11**

Here is how you can receive Christ:

1. Admit that you are a sinner.

   "All have sinned and fall short of the glory of God." **Romans 3:23**

2. Understand that the penalty of sin is death or eternal separation from God in hell.

   "For the wages of sin is death…" **Romans 6:23**

3. Believe that Jesus paid that price for us and offers us eternal life in heaven.

   "…but the gift of God is eternal life in Christ Jesus our Lord." **Romans 6:23**

4. Through prayer, invite Jesus to take control of your life through the Holy Spirit.

   "For everyone who calls on the name of the Lord will be saved." **Romans 10:13**

"To all who received Him, to those who believed in His name, He gave the right to become children of God." **John 1:12**

"I give them eternal life, and they shall never perish; no one can snatch them out of my hand." **John 10:28**

Section 2

The Sheep of His Pasture

"Shout for joy to the Lord, all the earth. Worship the Lord with gladness; come before Him with joyful songs. Know that the Lord is God. It is He who made us, and we are His; we are His people, the sheep of His pasture."

"Enter His gates with thanksgiving and His courts with praise; give thanks to Him and praise His name. For the Lord is good and His love endures forever; His faithfulness continues through all generations."

Psalm 100

Introduction

Imagine a land where the difference between the blistering heat of summer and the brutal cold of winter can span a range of 150 degrees. That place is central South Dakota. That is where I live. Our home for over 30 years was a small farm where my husband Paul and I raised our three children, Philip, April and Gina, and eventually also entertained in-laws and grandchildren. Our farm became home to a wide variety of animals, some of whom were pets and others who were just part of farm production. But each of these animals touched our lives in one way or another.

For 22 years sheep grazed our pastures in the summer and filled our barn with song in the winter. These amazing wooly creatures started out to be just a project that would hopefully help pay a few bills. However, very quickly we discovered that they were much more. They became a big part of our conversations, dreams, child-rearing and adventures. We quickly learned that God had great things to teach us through them about Himself, ourselves, and about life. He opened our eyes to some truths He taught in the Bible using these humble friends.

For sheep farmers here in South Dakota, in the middle of the winter season comes another season: lambing season. It is a time when the barn echoes with the sound of tiny voices from the precious lambs. Even the hardest heart has a tender spot for those little babies. It was a time that we looked forward to with eager anticipation each winter, although it was filled with a great deal of hard work and sometimes disappointments. Each of these seasons brought new stories to tell and lambs to remember.

We all, like sheep, have gone astray. Each of us has turned to his own way; and the Lord has laid on Him (Jesus) the iniquity (sin) of us all. **Isaiah 53:6** *(parentheses mine)*

Chapter 1
The Shepherd in Training

I was first introduced to the wonderful world of woolies when I was an early teen. Having lived on this farm since I was six years old, we had always raised cattle; however, my dad, never shying away from a new venture, decided that sheep were the way to go for us and bought a small flock. This was going to be great! About that same time, I recall having an assignment in school requiring us to write a limerick. Mine went like this:

There once was a farmer named Mel
Who thought he'd like sheep very well.
But he came to his senses
When they climbed through his fences
And his wife and four kids hollered, "SELL!"

Fortunately, he didn't listen to his wife and four kids, and sheep became a part of our lives. My three siblings and

I each had his or her own sheep with high hopes for twins or even triplets come spring lambing time. I recall the anticipation as we learned to watch the signs alerting us to the approaching birth. Through those events we learned about new life as well as the reality of death as we soon discovered both were a part of caring for animals on the farm.

One of my favorite pastimes was to sit on the fence in the barn or in the feed trough and be with the lambs. They gathered around me and I would make up stories to tell them or just tell them my teenager troubles. Sometimes I taught them Bible stories or sang to them. But no matter what I did, what eventually impressed me most was that they were so content just to be in my presence. They would all gather around me closely, some touching me while others timidly backed away a step or two, and they would just stand there quietly for as long as I stayed with them.

I think so often back to those times and cannot help but marvel how that is the kind of intimate relationship God desires to have with me. I have often longed for that true joy, peace and quietness, and the contentment that only comes at the feet of Jesus. Instead, however, I bustle headlong into my day, not taking the time to listen to Him or just savor His presence. What a picture of the kind of trust and love relationship He longs to have with me.

"You have made known to me the path of life; You will fill me with joy in Your presence, with eternal pleasures at your right hand." **Psalm 16:11**

"You will keep in perfect peace him whose mind is steadfast, because he trusts in You." **Isaiah 26:3**

Chapter 2
The Practice Field

Time passed. I went off to college, married and had three beautiful children; and in 1987 my husband Paul and I moved to our farm where we now live. The next spring of 1988 we bought our first flock of sheep.

Before I go any further, I must break for a little terminology lesson for those not privileged to have grown up with such wooly friends. Ewe (pronounced "you") is a female sheep and a buck is a male.

Paul had not been around sheep before so was in for an education. That first flock consisted of 23 "short-term" ewes. These were sheep which, at a ripe old age of 8 or 9, were due for retirement from productivity. Their teeth were bad, their strength was waning, and their health was marginal, but they were due to offer one more generation of lambs in a month or so. These poor wooly ladies did not realize that the hands they were trusting were the hands of novices. They needed a lot of extra care, but they provided for us the ewe lambs which became the backbone of a wonderful flock that lasted for years to come.

Friends, we are never too old, too frail, too limited to be useful and productive for our Shepherd, Jesus Christ. Even in our weakness, may we be able to say,

> *"My flesh and my heart may fail, but God is the strength of my heart and my portion forever."* **Psalm 73:26**

He has a purpose for each life to the end so that we can say with the Apostle Paul,

> *"...I consider my life worth nothing to me, if only I may finish the race and complete the task the Lord Jesus has given me – the task of testifying to the gospel of God's grace."* **Acts 20:24**

Chapter 3
The Flock

Sheep have personalities just like people do, and the more time one spends with them the more evident those personalities become. Some are trusting and others are timid and distant. Some are leaders, both good and bad, and some are followers. Some are compliant and easy to work with. Others are… well, those are the ones that give sheep a bad rap and make the wife and four kids holler "SELL!" Sounds a little like people? The apostle Paul says in 1 Corinthians 11:1, *"Follow my example, as I follow the example of Christ."*

Let me introduce a few friends from our flock who provided illustrations of such an example.

Aggie

One such personality I want to introduce you to was Aggie. Aggie was a large tame ewe who had probably been someone's pet before she came to our farm. She loved to be with us. Aggie would follow us wherever we went even if all the other sheep went the other way. She was not afraid to stand alone—if she could stand with the shepherd. We often relied on her to lead the rest of the flock to the desired location.

One day we needed to separate some sheep from the rest of the flock, but the sheep were quite some distance from the yard out in the tree strip. In South Dakota, where the wind can do its damage with erosion or blizzards, we plant several rows of trees close together in a long strip, hence the name tree strip. This acts as a wind block to slow the wind or catch the snow. Our tree strip is L-shaped with a fence and gate across the corner of it. The grass was tall and thick there so we were allowing our sheep to graze it. The goal was to sort the sheep so that the younger ones were in one leg of the L and the older ones in the other leg with a fence and gate separating the two.

Our faithful Aggie followed us as we walked through the flock and out the gate. Each time some followed her, and we were able to let some pass and redirect others. Then we led her through again, and still more would follow her. In that way we were able to completely sort the sheep without even needing a corral.

Another time a gate had been left open and the whole flock had wandered across the yard and into our alfalfa field which was tall and ready to be mowed for hay. Alfalfa is like candy to these grasslovers because it is similar in effect to a child gorging on candy with the resulting miserable belly ache. Once we noticed them there, we had only to call Aggie's name. She quickly ran to us with the others close behind, and we together led the flock back to their home.

In the same way, God asks us to be trusting followers of our Shepherd. In Matthew 16:24 Jesus said to His disciples, *"If anyone desires to come after me, let him deny himself and take up his cross and follow Me."* To deny oneself is to follow Christ even when all the other sheep are going the other direction.

Such followers were Joshua and Caleb when the 12 spies were sent to scout out the promised land (Numbers 13-14). Ten spies brought back negative reports based on their evaluation of their strength. Joshua and Caleb brought back positive reports based on the promises and faithfulness of

God and His power. Of them God said in Numbers 14:24, *"But my servant Caleb, because he has a different spirit in him and has followed Me fully, I will bring into the land where he went, and his descendants will inherit it."* Fellow sheep, do not be afraid to stand alone as long as you are following Christ the Shepherd. He holds all the power and has already won the battle.

I have witnessed young people being willing to stand alone against the tide of peer pressure and worldly standards so they could be obedient to following Christ the Shepherd. God is the rewarder of those who seek Him.

> *"Don't let anyone look down on you because you are young, but set an example for the believers in speech, in life, in love, in faith and in purity."*
> **1 Timothy 4:12**

Rose

Rose was one of our original 23 ewes who made up the practice field for our sheep-raising adventure. Her personality could be labeled as inquisitive, happy, curious, endearing. She had a very unique routine of always wanting to sniff the face of anyone who would allow such a personal encounter. (If you have ever been up close and personal with an animal which picks that moment to sneeze, you understand the potential for this affectionate act to be less than appealing, especially in the dead of winter!) She would stretch up as high as she could and even stand on the fence in order to reach the friendly face before her. We never really guessed what pleasure she found in her sniffing, but her persistence earned her the name The Nose which evolved to Rose Nose and eventually just Rose. Rose was a delight to work with, always cheerful and cooperative.

> *"They will receive blessing from the LORD and vindication from God their Savior. Such is the generation of those who seek Him, who seek Your face, O God."* **Psalm 24:5-6**

Another pleasant member of our sheep family was Olga. She came to us a few years into our experience. She was one of those quiet unassuming ewes who could easily go unnoticed as she called no special attention to herself, as did Rose. But she earned a special spot in our hearts one spring as the wooly lady who would accept any orphan.

As I have stated before, life and death are both factors to be reckoned with while raising animals. This particular morning, we had a ewe that had died while giving birth, but we were there at that moment to rescue her unborn lamb. After some serious CPR applied to this newly delivered baby, he coughed and sputtered and decided to give life a try.

Olga was nearby having given birth to a single lamb a few hours earlier. Even though we knew that a mother ewe usually ferociously rejects a baby other than her own, we decided to try putting this newborn with Olga to see if she would accept him. She was gentle and maternal, so it just might work. To our great pleasure, she immediately began licking and cleaning up this little orphan while uttering the soft gentle murmurs understood only between a mama sheep and her baby. In years to come we frequently called on her to raise an orphan, and she won her place on our "wool" of fame.

(Pardon the pun!)

"For the LORD your God...defends the cause of the orphan and the widow, and loves the alien, giving him food and clothing." **Deuteronomy 10:18**

Number 39

All of our sheep were given a plastic tag in their ear with a number on it. This was our main means of identification of them for record keeping purposes. As we got to know their personalities better, many of them earned names as those whose stories are told above. However, some of them have been stored equally special as numbers in our memories. Our favorite undoubtedly was number 39. She was the daughter of one of our "first 23" and chosen as a lamb to be kept for production purposes. I am not really sure why we decided to keep her. She was very small and did not necessarily exhibit many of the desirable traits of a breeding ewe—tall, long body, deep heavy frame. She was fine-boned and short. A reject by economic standards. However, she had a lesson to teach us.

It is possible, though not usually desirable, for a young ewe to give birth by the time it passes its first birthday. Sheep ranchers will tell of the frustrations of working with those first-time young moms as they may reject their babies, have inadequate milk supply for their baby, and often lack many important maternal instincts. Our #39 was pregnant, however, and ready to give birth. Her belly was huge, so we anticipated that we would have bottle lambs out of this deal. What a surprise when she gave birth to triplets! Seldom do these young ewes have more than one the first time, but triplets were definitely unexpected. Even more unexpected, however, was her willingness to accept all three and give them the maternal care they needed.

It is important to understand that ewes come equipped with a table set for two but definitely not three. Very rarely can they support three lambs. The weakest will be pushed away and allowed to starve if the shepherd does not intervene and feed it with a bottle. But #39, even in her rather immature condition and with her stature deficit, fed and raised all three of those lambs.

That alone would be an accomplishment worth mentioning. But in the eight years that we had #39, and that is quite a few years for a sheep, she raised triplets every year. Do the math. That little sheep, the one most economic-minded producers would have rejected, produced around 24 lambs for us.

God used her to teach us that God does not look at greatness the way we do. When looking for God's chosen king for Israel, the one who would eventually be in the genealogic line of our Savior Jesus Christ, God chose David, a young boy and a lowly shepherd instead of his seven older, taller, politically-correct brothers. God said of each brother,

> *"Do not consider his appearance or his height, for I have rejected him. The LORD does not look at the things man looks at. Man looks at the outward appearance, but the LORD looks at the heart."*
> **1 Samuel 16:7.**

Remember that it is the power of God that works in us, not our own. John 15:5: ***"I am the vine and you are the branches. If a man remains in me and I in him, he will bear much fruit; apart from me you can do nothing."***

In stark contrast to #39 were those ewes which stopped producing lambs. Just as in John chapter 15, they were cut off (culled) and sold for slaughter as they were not beneficial for anyone else and hurt productivity. Jesus also cuts off every branch that bears no fruit but prunes a life given over to Him so that it will be even more fruitful. I am so thankful that He cares enough about us to prune away the bad habits and attitudes that drag us down, get us off the track, and distract our focus from the One who is our strength.

Each of us is here for a purpose that was set into motion at the creation of the world. Ephesians 2:10 NLT: *"For we are God's masterpiece. He has created us anew in Christ Jesus, so we can do the good things He planned for us long ago."* It is no accident you and I were born at this appointed time and each of us has a mission in this world. Jesus gives us all we need to accomplish His purposes if we are willing to let Him. Glory to God!

Squirt

If you are reading this portion of this book, you probably already met and fell in love with Squirt as we did. I know God smiled when he brought Squirt into the world that cold March evening knowing His purposes for the tiny lamb. No life is without great value to our Shepherd. The Bible is full of the phrase "at the appointed time…" Those words are a great comfort to me when I realize God has it all in His control, in His mighty hands.

Also, I have learned to keep my eyes open for "God sightings." I am eternally thankful that God is at work all around me, every minute of every day. He delights to reveal Himself to those who have *"eyes to see and ears to hear,"*

(Matthew 13:16). I pray for God to open my eyes to what He is doing around me so I can be ready and alert to join Him and give Him praise.

Chapter 4
The Lessons Learned

Hey, I know that voice!

Over the years our family has been constantly blessed by passages of scripture which have come alive before our eyes. They may be familiar ones to us that take on new meaning when the actors take the stage and bring the script to life. Sometimes these lessons have made us laugh, sometimes cry, and sometimes just shake our heads in amazement.

> *"¹I tell you the truth, the man who does not enter the sheep pen by the gate, but climbs in by some other way, is a thief and a robber. ²The man who enters by the gate is the shepherd of his sheep. ³The watchman opens the gate for him, and the sheep listen to his voice. He calls his own sheep by name and leads them out. ⁴When he has brought out all his own, he goes on ahead of them, and his sheep follow him because they know his voice. ⁵But they will never follow a stranger; in fact, they will run*

away from him because they do not recognize a stranger's voice." **John 10:1-5**

We talk to our sheep a lot and, just like this passage says, they learn which voice to listen to and follow and which to ignore. One year, early in our experience with sheep, shearing day had come. Our shearers had arrived before we were quite ready and they were getting their gear in place. We had to move the sheep from the barn over to another building that they were not very familiar with. As always, we called to them and the heavy-fleeced pets were cautiously following us into these less-than-familiar surroundings. Our shearers finished their preparations and entered the barnyard by another gate. When our timid sheep saw them and heard their unfamiliar voices, they behaved exactly as these verses said they would. They quickly fled retreating back to the security of the barn. The experienced sheep shearers soon disappeared and the wary flock once again followed us to the shearing pad.

Paul and I worked with middle school children at our church, our favorite age group. On one occasion we arranged to bring our youth group to our farm for a field trip. March was our lambing month, and we wanted them to be able to experience firsthand the truths of Bible passages such as the one above. Before we entered the barn where the moms with babies were penned, we told them about these verses. We related to them the story above and urged them to be very quiet. As we entered the barn these teens were respectfully quiet and the sheep were not confused by their presence at all as they only heard the shepherd voices.

In this world today many voices around us are telling us how to find happiness, peace and fulfillment. There are voices ringing out deceitful messages about how to be all that we can be and what success looks like. Voices try to convince us this is truth, or here is the way to truth, or that truth is what is right for me. The thief screams out deception that eternal life in heaven is for those who are good enough, or at least better than the ones we sneer at beneath our upturned noses. It is confusing and the sheep scatter. But if we spend time with the Shepherd, listening to His voice through the Bible, He speaks to us and we come to know Him, His voice, and His truth. Then when we hear the stranger's voice we will have discernment and not confusion. Verses 7 through 9 of John 10 say, *"...All who ever came before me were thieves and robbers, but the sheep did not listen to them. I am the gate; whoever enters through me will be saved (or have eternal life)."* (Parentheses mine.)

Follow the Leader

> *"I will lead the blind by ways they have not known, along unfamiliar paths I will guide them; I will turn the darkness into light before them and make the rough places smooth. These are the things I will do; I will not forsake them."* **Isaiah 42:16**

Another spiritual lesson was brought home one spring. Our pasture is a long rectangle with a creek bed completely crossing it near the far north end. Usually that creek bed is empty, but in the early spring after the thaw it can have a foot or two of water in it. Of course, the grass on the far side of that creek is best—lush and more tender than that on the near side. It seems that is where we find ourselves often, imagining how good it must be over there somewhere with this great obstacle separating us from our desires. Sometimes, however, God uses that obstacle to protect us from the dangers that He sees but we do not. That is true for our sheep also. In the spring sheep are a delicacy on the menu for coyotes striving to feed their young. Sheep have poor eyesight and are quite defenseless. Therefore, a trapped sheep is easy prey. For that reason, we want them to stay on the home side of the creek so they can come home to the safety of the barnyard at night.

One day, however, they ventured across that creek somehow, and we had to figure out how to get them to come back across. We walked out to the creek and called to them again and again. They wanted to come but could not figure out how to get back across. We bribed them with a pail of corn. They paced back and forth on the opposite bank about 20 feet across the water but just could not bring themselves to step into the unknown of the water before them. Finally, we decided we would have to show them the way. I took off my shoes, rolled up my pant legs, walked through the water to the other side, turned around and came right back. Those silly sheep followed right behind me staying within the ripples left by my steps.

Paul and I laughed at them as we thought of the spiritual significance of that sight. Isaiah 30:21 promises the Israelites that if they would obey God, *"Whether you turn to the right or to the left, your ears will hear a voice behind you saying, 'This is the way, walk in it.'"* Our loving heavenly Shepherd promises in Proverbs 4:11: *"I will guide you in the way of wisdom and lead you along straight paths."*

The Sound of Silence

"He (Jesus) was oppressed and afflicted, yet He did not open his mouth; He was led like a lamb to the slaughter, and as a sheep before her shearers is silent, so He did not open His mouth." **Isaiah 53:7b**

It seems that when there is no purpose at all for such chatter sheep will just bawl their heads off, like when we walk out the door of our house and our wooly friends see us. They all start in with their verbal raucous…as if we didn't know they were there? Do they really think supper will be served more quickly if they make more noise?

However, there are definitely times when they are silent. Times of fear or uncertainty. Times of helplessness. Times of great distress.

Once a year we remove that heavy coat of wool which is eventually sold, cleaned, dyed, weaved, and placed on the store shelf in the form of socks, coats, sweaters and pants. At shearing time, we tip the sheep off her feet so she sits on her rump. Up to that moment the sheep fights with all the strength she can muster to avoid being caught. While no more painful than a haircut, the idea of being restrained in any way is worth the fight. But as soon as the handler has her off her feet the fight is gone and she is silent. (My sheep shearer is shaking his head right now saying, "Oh yeah?" Okay, they sometimes still try to stage a couple of revolts but will give up for the most part.) As long as she cannot get her feet beneath her, she is willing to endure in silence whatever is before her. Sheep do not open their mouths in rebellion and stay silent.

So was Jesus' example as he faced the cross and all it entailed. The oppression and affliction He endured in that immeasurable act of love for us is incomprehensible. Yet He did not fight back with His mouth or His might. He entrusted his life to His Father in heaven to complete the purpose that was before Him. *Let us fix our eyes on Jesus, the author and perfecter of our faith, who for the joy set before Him endured the cross, scorning its shame, and sat down at the right hand of the throne of God.* Hebrews 12:2

Sometimes the only way God gets me to stop fighting His work in my life is to knock me off my feet. As long as I am functioning in the scope of my own power, I will constantly be at war with my Savior and what He wants to do in and through my life. He knows that, as His sheep, the best way to get me to stop fighting is sometimes to pull my legs out from under me. Then He can refine me into a lamb He can use and bless. When I am quiet I can hear Him say to me, ***"Be still and know that I am God."*** Psalm 46:10. Can you identify?

Being led to slaughter is also a time when sheep are silently led to face the outcome. We had a ewe some years back that was very difficult – the type who made the wife and four kids holler "SELL!" On a daily basis she was out of her pen, jumping fences, and getting into trouble at every opportunity. It would be safe to say that she was not our favorite! Finally, we made the decision that she would be better off served with potatoes and corn than to have to battle with her in this way. My husband happily loaded her into our pickup box before going to work so I could take her to the butcher in town. My spirit was light as I drove out of the yard thinking how nice it would be not to have to deal with her ever again.

I made the mistake of looking in my rear-view mirror to make sure she had not jumped out of there too. There I met her eyes, deep brown, sad, remorseful even. She just kept watching me – in silence. The trip to town takes about 20 minutes, and in that time my eyes were continually drawn to hers in my mirror. She seemed so helpless and scared. By the time I got her to town I could not even unload her. I just walked away from the pickup and let the butcher take her away. Fortunately, I got over it quickly and enjoyed her as a tasty entrée.

Take Care of My Sheep

"Be shepherds of God's flock that is under your care...not lording it over those entrusted to you, but being examples to the flock." **I Peter 5:2-3**

"Keep watch over yourselves and all the flock of which the Holy Spirit has made you overseers. Be shepherds of the church of God." **Acts 20:28**

Often during our sheep-raising years Paul and I commented that we think if a person really wants to be a pastor or teacher or just a servant to people, he or she should be required to complete an internship with a farmer or rancher through lambing season. In South Dakota, besides the seasons of winter, spring, summer and fall, we have fishing season, hunting season, hay fever season, and, if one raises sheep, there is lambing season. In most cases it extends from a month before those adorable little babies appear on the scene to about the time they are loaded on the truck on sale day. During that time is when the shepherd's abilities are put to the test. Anything and everything can happen and usually does. This testing ground can all be summed up in the saying, "Anybody can throw corn in the trough, but it takes a shepherd to keep the lambs alive." Let me illustrate.

One particular spring we had a fine flock of three-month-old lambs. They had just been weaned and all seemed well. But one morning I noticed one little fellow who just moved to the side when the others crowded around the trough for a meal. His ears drooped a little and his belly seemed rather bloated. He nibbled a bit at the feed but obviously had little appetite for the life-sustaining food. Occasionally I saw him grunt and strain a little, but it did not seem serious so I went on about my business.

A couple of days passed by with little change in this distressed little guy. He was not getting worse but neither was he improving. Finally, I stopped and really took account of what was going on with him. After a few minutes of studying his lackluster behavior, I mused that if I was acting like that I would probably be constipated! I determined that since sheep are so much like humans, and this one was not looking like it wanted to live very long in this condition, it was worth taking the chance on my hunch. So I concocted a slurry of milk of magnesia and water and gave Junior a drink. The next morning, I went out to visit my patient. He was eating like he was making up for lost meals and skipping around with his friends. The pot-belly was gone, and I am positive he even smiled at me a little.

Another "patient" of mine taught me that the Heimlich is not only for humans. Immediately after giving birth to their lambs, ewes have a ravenous appetite. We fed them hay but avoided feeding them any grain for even up to 24 hours after lambing because they tend to eat so fast that they can inhale the grain and choke. As a child I witnessed a scene which will be forever etched in my mind as a ewe who inhaled her corn choked to death as I watched helplessly. I promised myself I would never let that happen again if I could help it.

This particular evening, however, I recognized the shaking of the head, foaming at the mouth and thrashing body of a ewe which had eaten too quickly and inhaled her feed. As panic threatened to set in for me, I thought about how "human" these lowly creatures truly seem and the above lamb incident popped into my mind. "If the Heimlich maneuver can work for a person, maybe it can work for my sheep," I pondered.

I quickly jumped into her pen, wrapped my arms around her still-swollen belly and, finding the end of her rib cage, forced my fists upward into what I hoped was her diaphragm. No response. Subsequently, I repeated this procedure with a little more force, and the ball of lodged feed shot across the pen and splattered onto the floor. Success! She coughed a couple of airway-clearing coughs and went back to chewing her cud, what was left of it, unaware of her close encounter with death and the elated hero who stood at her side.

Yes, anybody can throw feed in the trough, but the sheep will still perish unless there is one who cares about them enough to get to know them. We sheep think we are pretty good at hiding our pain or whatever stressors may be going on in our lives. And we can do that pretty successfully if no one cares, if no one takes the time to watch and listen and ask questions. Eventually in our flock, we knew the sheep well enough to know their distinct behavior and personalities. We could tell by the drooping ears, disinterest in food, or isolation from others that there was a problem. If we cared enough to get involved, there was almost always a positive outcome.

The verses in John 21:15-17 always puzzled me until we learned this lesson. Here Jesus asked Peter, "Do you truly love me?" to which Peter replied, "Of course I do; you know that I do." This exchange occurred three times to which Jesus always responded with "Feed my lambs, …Take care of my sheep, …Feed my sheep." I am sure there is a lot of meaning here that I do not fully understand, but the importance of not merely feeding but actually caring for the flock was paramount.

I must add a humorous side note to this passage. Paul quickly made use of the very basic lesson taught here. When it was getting to be close to chore time, he often asked our children, "Do you love me?" "Of course," came their flippant reply. Paul's response: "Feed my sheep!" I recall that they caught on to that one rather quickly.

The Under-Shepherd

"Be shepherds of God's flock that is under your care, watching over them—not because you must, but because you are willing, as God wants you to be; not pursuing dishonest gain, but eager to serve." **1 Peter 5:2**

An "under-shepherd" refers to someone who serves under the authority of a "chief shepherd." Think of pastors and elders, teachers, parents, anyone given responsibility to oversee the flock of Christ. We also eventually had an under-shepherd for our flock for the times when we were not present with them.

Our pony, Shadow, was born shortly after our first 23 came to live at our farm. From the time he was a colt, the sheep had been his friends and companions, and he soon figured out that he was in charge! I am pretty sure he did not even realize he was not one of them but definitely accepted that he had a responsibility to protect them. He eventually became very possessive of his position as their guardian as even when Paul and I tried to walk among them he ran between us and his flock.

The Sheep of His Pasture

One summer night a heavy rain storm moved in and dropped eight inches of rain on our tiny spot in this world in only about an hour. Shadow and the sheep were in the pasture that night. By morning, when we went out to do our chores, we could see that the pasture was completely flooded. Deep concern flooded our minds as we recalled sheep are blind in the dark and also unable to swim with heavy fleece. But—Shadow to the rescue! He had led our sheep to the only dry spot left in the pasture, a shallow knoll about 20 feet across and against a fence. We cut the fence and led them back home to the barn with treats for our faithful pony.

Jesus, our Chief Shepherd, has not left us alone without undershepherds here on earth. I am so grateful for those pastors, elders, teachers and ministers who serve the flock in our churches, as well as parents who take spiritual nurturing of their children as a high calling. God has given them to us as earthly shepherds with the charge to lead, teach, and guard our souls. Be comforted knowing Jesus never leaves the sheep of His pasture alone!

The 99 Plus One

"Then Jesus told them this parable, 'Suppose one of you has a hundred sheep and loses one of them. Does he not leave the ninety-nine in the open country and go after the lost sheep until he finds it? And when he finds it, he joyfully puts it on his shoulders and goes home. Then he calls his friends and neighbors together and says, 'Rejoice with me; I have found my lost sheep.' I tell you, there is rejoicing in the presence of the angels of God over one sinner who repents.'" **Luke 15:4-6, 10**

Recently someone asked me, "Is that true? Would a shepherd really leave the 99 and go after one to rescue it?" I answered, "Absolutely. The one alone would not last for a night if it were not found and saved."

We had one particular lamb who insisted on putting its head through the small squares of a woven wire fence. I am sure that the greener taller grass held a temptation this lamb consistently did not resist. But getting into trouble is always easier than getting out of trouble. In the evening when we called the rest of the sheep to come to the barn we could hear a distant distress call from this stubborn lamb. We definitely left the "99" to go rescue the one. Within a few hours coyotes would have been enjoying a captive meal. I must note, however, that the rest of the flock was safe and secure while we went on such a rescue mission. The same is true for the truth behind this parable. When I trusted in Christ to be my Shepherd He put the Holy Spirit as Guard over my soul (John 10:28). I am never alone. To our supernatural and omnipresent (present always and everywhere) Savior, each individual is valued, and He will go to great lengths to rescue those who are lost while we are safe in His hands. Praise Him!

The Thief

"The thief comes only to steal and kill and destroy; I have come that they may have life, and have it to the fullest." **John 10:10**

Where we live the greatest "thief" of our sheep is the coyote. Sheep are nearly blind in the dark of night, which is no secret to predators who come in the darkest moments to steal away the vulnerable unaware victims. A friend of ours, whose job it is to help ranchers control the predator problem, told us that when a coyote attacks a sheep it bites the throat to suffocate it. Devouring the heart is one of its first goals. The "thief" in our lives comes in the form of temptation, distraction, anyone or anything that steals our joy and focus and goes against our abundant life through Christ. Like a coyote, the devil seeks to steal our hearts and minds away from the one true Shepherd who can give us life to the fullest.

Only once were our sheep unprotected in the pasture at night as Shadow, our pony, was to be trained to be ridden. Within a very short time a coyote killed one and seriously injured another which escaped. With much tender care the injured ewe survived and eventually rejoined the flock. After that night we never left them unprotected as our pony, who thought he was one of them, was allowed to resume his post as their fierce guardian.

The Sheep Without a Shepherd

"Jesus traveled through all the towns and villages in that area, teaching in the synagogues and announcing the Good News about the Kingdom. And He healed every kind of disease and illness. When He saw the crowds, he had compassion on them, because they were confused and helpless, like sheep without a shepherd."

Matthew 9:35-36 NLT

The Sheep of His Pasture

A sheep without a shepherd equals a dangerous situation. As in previous illustrations, this leaves a sheep vulnerable to attack and wandering in confusion. Sheep always want a leader. As I have mentioned, some are good leaders and others not so much. Our sheep made that poor choice one day and followed another through a weak spot in the fence. Soon all of them were on the other side in unfamiliar territory. They wandered aimlessly for about a half mile until they came to another farm. That neighbor called us to report the strays. We found them circling, uncertain which way to turn, and afraid of everything.

Their relief was visible as soon as we called to them and they lined up to follow. We led them back to our farm and the security of our green pastures.

Unlike cattle, sheep cannot be driven, they must be led. Attempting to force or drive sheep results in them circling as none of them wants to take the lead. But they will quickly follow the leader they know. Our human challenge is to know our Shepherd so well that we distinguish between His voice and that of the deceiver, and learn to trust His sovereign loving hand.

Firstfruits

"Honor the Lord with your wealth, with the firstfruits of all your crops; then your barns will be filled to overflowing, and your vats will brim over with new wine." **Proverbs 3:9-10**

Not every lesson we learned from our sheep-raising experience came wrapped up in a cute fluffy white package. One lesson was particularly hard but never to be forgotten. Make no mistake, God does not always reinforce his teachings in life quite so vividly as this, but maybe He knew we needed a visual, and maybe it happened for such a book as this.

From the beginning of our marriage, we had tithed to the Lord. It really was not something we had to think too hard about. However, for reasons we no longer recall, one year when our biggest lambs were ready to be sold, we decided that we needed the money these lambs would produce and we would tithe our second-string lambs when the time came. Fifty lambs had been born this year, more than in any other year. Five lambs were big enough to sell so we planned on taking them to market the next day. Our needs would be met.

The Sheep of His Pasture

Shock took our breath away the next morning when we entered the barn and found our five big lambs dead on the floor. Remember how much we are like sheep? Gluttony and greed run rampant in sheep as well as humanity. The biggest ones push the smaller ones aside and gorge on the feed until they have overeaten. This creates a toxic overload reaction in their digestive system that kills them quickly. Another lesson learned the hard way. But we immediately connected this tragedy to a concept we had read in God's word. Obedience to God comes first.

"Bring the whole tithe into the storehouse…test me in this," says the Lord Almighty, "and see if I will not throw open the floodgates of heaven and pour out so much blessing that you will not have room enough for it. I will prevent pests from devouring your crops, and the vines in your fields will not lose their fruit." **Malachi 3:10-11**

We cannot out-give God. He promises in Philippians 4:19, ***"And this same God who takes care of me will supply all your needs from His glorious riches, which have been given to us in Christ Jesus."*** (NLT) God did take care of our needs in His own way because no bill went unpaid and we were not left in need. And these many years later we do not even remember why we chose to put ourselves before God. But His mercies never fail and He continues to bless our obedience to Him.

We know of a couple who had carefully saved enough to replace their aging roof when the time came. But in the meantime, they became aware of a serious and expensive life-changing need of a friend. Believing God was prompting them to give their repair money to this need, they chose to trust Him. Through God's blessing, this life was changed. Almost exactly one year after making the decision to obey, a hail storm finished off their ailing roof and insurance coverage completely replaced the roof at a cost of $3000 more than they had saved. Their barn was full to overflowing!

Chapter 5
The Shepherd's Psalm

At this point, I hope Psalm 23 takes on new meaning for all of us. This is my personal reflection. I am thankful God has given us this picture of His heart.

The Lord is my Shepherd, I shall not be in want. He is fully aware of and capable of providing every need I have.

He makes me lie down in green pastures, He leads me beside quiet waters, He restores my soul. Sheep lie down when they feel a sense of contentment, security, peace and fullness. I can enjoy that same gift when I know He's in control and watching over me.

He guides me in paths of righteousness for His name's sake. He is my all-knowing Guide. I can trust Him to choose the path for me that will glorify His name.

Even though I walk through the valley of the shadow of death, I will fear no evil, for You are with me; Your rod

and Your staff, they comfort me. I know there will be times of great uncertainty in my life and fear will want to take over, but I trust my Shepherd to always be right there with me to hold my hand and lead me through.

You prepare a table before me in the presence of my enemies. You anoint my head with oil; my cup overflows. The Shepherd is my shelter and my source of strength when the thief comes through another gate trying to lead me astray. The Shepherd is always waiting with the healing oil of forgiveness when I fail. Then my cup once again overflows with joy.

Surely goodness and love will follow me all the days of my life, and I will dwell in the house of the Lord forever. Heavenly Shepherd, all my life You have been so good. I rest knowing You love me always. Thank You for salvation and the promise that I will be with You forever in heaven.

Amen.

Chapter 6
The Big Question

The million-dollar question is, "How can I know God's voice? How can I be sure it is His voice and not just my own thoughts and desires I am listening to?"

I have spent my life struggling with that question. I believe every person who comes to know Christ as Savior and Shepherd feels the same. Through our experiences with sheep, and the journey of life as a whole, a few insights have aided us in this walk with Christ.

A few times we purchased ewes from Wyoming where they had been raised in more of a hands-off situation. Those were the sheep who had never been in a barn or been in up-close-and-personal contact with a shepherd. In many situations a dog was the protector of the flock. Therefore, they arrived at our small farm with many fears and great mistrust of humans. This posed many challenges, not the least of which was how to get them to trust our voices and presence. This timid group would be kept close to the barn where we would walk among them very often so they could get used to our voices and mannerisms and we could get to know them.

In the same way, talking often with God and telling Him everything weighing on my heart helps me feel comfortable with revealing myself to Him, and prepares me to hear His voice. His words come through the Bible, God's Word. Psalms, Proverbs and the New Testament are full of the words God speaks to us through the Holy Spirit. We have been given this promise: ***But you have received the Holy Spirit, and He lives within you, so you don't need anyone to teach you what is true, for the Spirit teaches you everything you need to know, and what He teaches is true—it is not a lie. So just as He has taught you, remain in fellowship with Christ.*** 1 John 2:27

Recently a young woman asked my opinion about a moral issue. After a brief explanation of my belief, I urged her to not take my word for it but ask God to reveal His truth about it from the Bible. Then she would really know it was truth. So she studied and chose to follow God's leading.

Then she informed me she was urging her friends to do the same. What victory!

Thus, first, we must ask the Holy Spirit to teach us truth from the Bible and trust Him to do so as we read and pray. The more time I spend with God listening for His voice through the Bible, the more I will recognize His voice of Truth.

Second, we must know that God will never go against His Word. If what I think I am hearing is supported by what God says in Scripture, I can proceed with the assurance that it would be truth. Remember, the thief comes through another gate and deception can sound convincing, but there is always some part of it that does not line up with God's Word.

Third, confirmation that what I believe God is prompting me to do can come through others who I know to be close followers of Jesus. I have often asked God to confirm His leading through my husband or another trusted person. Personally, I often do not even tell another person what I think God is telling me to do, but then my husband or trusted friend brings it up and speaks the same idea to me. I ask others to pray with me about some decisions. Also Bible verses will continually "show up" in my study time that speak truth to my prayer concern.

I struggle memorizing Bible verses, but I keep cards with my favorite verses written on them near my Bible to read often. When big decisions have come my way, fragments of those verses flood my mind and I know they are the voice of the Shepherd. Then I can move forward with confidence as my trusted Shepherd leads.

All along the way, pray, pray, pray! I have become convinced that God loves to hear us say three little words: "I don't know." James 1:5 says, *"If any of you lacks wisdom, he should ask God, who gives generously to all without finding fault, and it will be given to you."* I believe God is delighted in us when we acknowledge our complete dependence on Him for then He can move in mighty and supernatural ways. Our faith is strengthened and He is glorified. *Trust in the Lord with all your heart and lean not on your own understanding. In all your ways acknowledge Him, and He will make your paths straight.* Proverbs 3:5-6

The Sheep of His Pasture

Praise be to Jesus!
He is the faithful Shepherd.
I love being loved by Him!

"I am the Good Shepherd. The Good Shepherd lays down His life for the sheep." **John 10:11**

"I am the Good Shepherd; I know my sheep and my sheep know me." **John 10:14**

www.ingramcontent.com/pod-product-compliance
Lightning Source LLC
Chambersburg PA
CBHW071538120626
46550CB00006B/2493